An I Can Read Book®

Magic
Secrets

REVISED EDITION

606105

by Rose Wyler and Gerald Ames

Pictures by Arthur Dorros

HarperTrophy
A Division of HarperCollinsPublishers

228746

MAGIC SECRETS
Text copyright © 1990 by Rose Wyler and Gerald Ames
Illustrations copyright © 1990 by Arthur Dorros

Library of Congress Cataloging-in-Publication Data
Wyler, Rose.
    Magic secrets / by Rose Wyler and Gerald Ames ; pictures by Arthur
Dorros. — Rev. ed.
        p.   cm. — (An I can read book)
    Summary: Easy magic tricks for the aspiring young magician.
    ISBN 0-06-026646-5 — ISBN 0-06-026647-3 (lib. bdg.)
    ISBN 0-06-444153-9 (pbk.)
    1. Conjuring—Juvenile literature.   2. Tricks—Juvenile
literature.   [1. Magic tricks.]   I. Ames, Gerald.   II. Dorros,
Arthur, ill.   III. Title   IV. Series.
GV1548.W85   1990   89-35841
793.8—dc20   CIP
                                                                      AC

REVISED EDITION
First Harper Trophy edition, 1991.

This is a book of magic tricks.

The tricks look hard,

but they are easy to do.

Try them and see.

Make a pencil disappear.

Push a glass through a table.

Pop a grape

through your head.

Surprise your friends

and make them laugh.

Be a magician!

HOW MAGIC WORKS

Meet Presto, the magician.

He shows you his hat.

It is empty, but wait....

5

Presto puts his hat on the table
and waves his magic wand.
He says a magic word—"*Abracadabra.*
Then he picks up his hat
and pulls out a rabbit!

Where was the rabbit?

It was in a black bag

behind the table.

When Presto picked up his hat,

he slipped the bag into it.

Then he pulled out the rabbit.

Presto says,

"I eat goldfish. Yum yum!"

He puts his hand into a fishbowl

and takes out a goldfish.

See it wiggle!

Presto pops the fish into his mouth.

Did Presto really eat a goldfish?

No, he ate a piece of carrot.

Presto had the carrot up his sleeve.

He let it drop into his hand.

He wiggled it and made you think

it was a goldfish.

That is how magic works.

The magician lets you see

only what he wants you to see.

He makes you think

what he wants you to think.

Presto fooled you—

he made you watch the wrong thing.

MAGIC TRICKS FOR YOU

Here are some magic tricks for you.

They are easy to do,

but you must practice them.

Practice the tricks in front of a mirror

to see how they look.

All magicians do this.

Talk while you do each trick.

Talking is very important.

You can make your friends laugh

and make them think

what you want them to think.

Then you can fool them.

Make a Pencil Disappear

Hold a pencil up.

Place a handkerchief over it.

Say, "Pencil, disappear!

Abracadabra."

Take away the handkerchief and—

the pencil is gone!

The secret:

As you cover the pencil,

hold up your finger.

Your finger holds up

the handkerchief.

The pencil drops into your lap.

But do not tell the secret.

Magicians never tell.

Rubber Pencil

"See this pencil," you say.

"I will turn it into rubber.

Abracadabra."

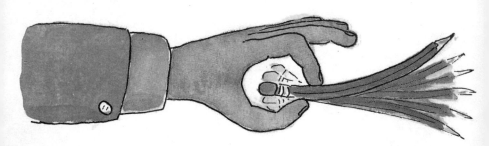

Then hold the pencil like this

and shake your hand up and down.

The pencil seems to bend like rubber.

To see how it looks,

do this trick in front of a mirror.

16

Turn Four Pennies into Five

Put four pennies on the table.

Push them into one hand

and close your hand.

Say "*Abracadabra.*"

Open your hand

and count the pennies.

There are five!

The secret:

First take some gum

and stick a penny

under the table.

As you push the four pennies

into your hand,

reach under the table

and pull off the other penny.

Tame an Egg

Ask your friends,

"Can you make an egg stand up?"

They try and try,

but the egg rolls over.

Say, "I will tame the egg.

Abracadabra. Egg, stand!"

You put the egg on the table and—

it stands!

The secret:

First put a little pile of salt

under the tablecloth.

The egg will stand in a pile of salt.

21

Make a Penny Disappear

Fold a piece of paper this way—
then unfold it.
Put the penny in the center.
Fold the paper again
with the penny inside.
Give the paper to a friend.
When he opens it,
the penny is gone!

The secret:

Fold the paper this way first.

Let the penny slip out

and fall into your lap.

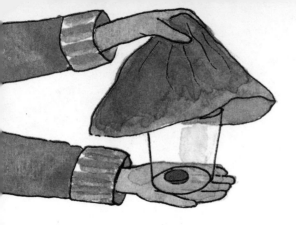

Good-bye, Penny

Say,

"Here is the penny that disappeared.

I will make it disappear again."

Show the penny in a glass—like this.

Then cover the glass with a cloth

and give the glass to a friend.

Your friend looks into it.

The penny is gone!

The secret:

When you show the penny,

it only *seems* to be in the glass.

It is really in your hand

under the glass.

Magic Hand

Say, "My hand is magic.

A spoon will stick to it."

The spoon is on the table.

Touch it, then lift your hand.

The spoon sticks to your hand!

The secret:

This is how you lift the spoon.

Do it quickly and no one

will guess the secret.

The Rope Trick

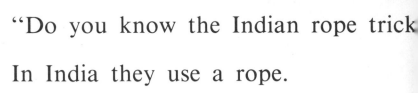

Say to your friends,

"Do you know the Indian rope trick

In India they use a rope.

I will use a thread.

This is much, much harder."

Rub a comb on your clothing.

Do it behind your back

so nobody will see.

Say, "Thread, stand up!"

Hold the comb over the thread.

The thread jumps up.

Say, "*Abracadabra*. Thread, dance!"

Move the comb, and the thread moves.

The secret:

Rubbing the comb gives it

a charge of electricity.

Write Through Your Hand

Say, "I will write through my hand.

First I make a mark here."

Mark your palm with ink.

Close your hand while the ink is wet.

30

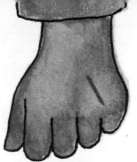

Then mark the back of your hand.

Say, "Mark, go through my hand

and make a cross on my palm."

Open your hand and—

there is a cross on your palm!

The secret:

Put the first mark in the right place,

and it makes a cross

when you close your hand.

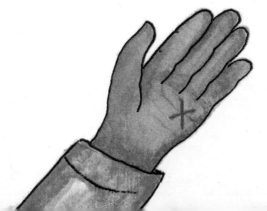

Genie in a Bottle

Show an empty bottle and a dime.

Wet the mouth of the bottle,

then put the dime on it.

Hold both hands on the bottle.

Say, "There is a genie in the bottle.

Genie, make the dime jump."

The dime starts jumping up and down.

CLICK—CLICK—CLICK!

The secret:

Use a cold bottle from the refrigerator.

The air in the bottle warms up,

and some pushes out.

This makes the dime jump

up and down.

Push a Glass Through a Table

Set a plastic glass on the table.

Take a piece of newspaper and say,

"I use paper so I won't hurt my hand

if the glass breaks."

Press the paper around the glass.

Hold up the paper

to show the glass is still inside.

Say,

"I put the glass back on the table."

Then push down on the paper.

Push and push until—

Bang! The glass hits the floor.

Does it really go through the table?

The secret:

After showing the glass in the paper,

let it slip into your lap.

Only the paper goes on the table.

Its shape fools your friends.

They think the glass is under it.

As you push down on the paper

let the glass fall

from your lap to the floor.

Do not tell the secret.

Magicians never tell.

Here are more magic tricks—

good ones for a show.

Practice them with a friend

who will be your helper.

For the show

dress up like a magician.

Use a ruler as a magic wand.

Have everything ready,

and it will be a great show.

Your Magic Wand

Hold up a little purse and say,
"My magic wand is in this purse."
Open the purse
and pull out a long ruler.

40

The secret:

First ask a grown-up

to cut a hole in the purse.

Have the ruler up your sleeve.

Push it into the hole.

Then open the purse

and pull out the ruler.

Wave the ruler and say,

"This is a real magic wand.

It can move by itself."

Push the ruler

into your closed hand.

Then hold up your hand

and the ruler begins to move.

It slowly rises from your hand.

The secret:

Slip a rubber band

over your finger.

It stretches

as you push the ruler down.

Then the rubber band

pulls the ruler up.

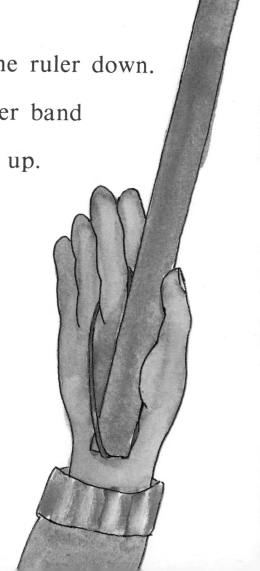

Penny, Come and Go

A glass stands upside down

on a sheet of white paper.

Put a penny on the paper.

Then take some newspaper

and roll it into a cone.

Cover the glass with the cone

and place the glass over the penny.

Say, "Penny, go away.

Abracadabra."

Take off the cone and—

the penny is gone!

Now say, "Penny, come back."

Again cover the glass with the cone.

Lift the glass and—

there is the penny!

The secret:

The secret is in the glass.

Paste white paper over the mouth.

It will not show when the glass

stands on a sheet of white paper.

The cone helps to hide the paper

on the glass.

When you set the glass over the penn

the paper hides the penny.

Human Magnet

Tell your friends,

"I am a magnet.

A penny will stick to me."

Press the penny on your forehead.

"*Abracadabra*. Penny, stick to me."

And the penny sticks.

The secret:

The penny stays there because

your skin is a little sticky.

Rope and Bottle

Show a plastic bottle and a rope.

Turn the bottle upside down.

Stick the rope in the bottle.

The rope hangs there by itself.

Then hold the rope up,

and the bottle hangs on the rope.

The secret:

Put a small ball of modeling clay
in the bottle.

The ball gets stuck in the bottle neck
and holds the rope there.

Cut a Lady in Half

Your lady is a paper doll.

You can make one yourself.

Then take a long envelope

and cut off the ends.

Put the doll in the envelope

so its head and feet stick out.

Say, "I will cut this lady in half."

You cut through the envelope.

Poor lady!

But wait....You pull it out and—

it is whole!

The secret:

Two slits are cut in the

back of the envelope.

The doll goes through the slits.

Then you can cut the envelope

but not the doll.

Mystery Marble

Show a marble in your hand,

then cover it with a handkerchief.

Say, "Feel under the handkerchief.

Is the marble still there?"

All your friends feel the marble.

It is still there.

Flick away the handkerchief and—

the marble is gone!

The secret:

The last one to feel the marble

is your helper.

He takes the marble away.

No one guesses the secret.

Then you cover your hand again.

Your friends all feel

under the handkerchief.

The marble is not there.

When you lift the handkerchief,

the marble is back.

Your helper was last again,

and he put it back.

Pop a Grape Through Your Head

Here is a funny trick.

All you need is a grape.

Well, two grapes,

but you just show one.

Say, "I'll pop this grape

right through my head."

Toss the grape from hand to hand.

"This helps get it ready," you say.

Raise your right hand

and smack the top of your head.

Open your mouth—

and out pops the grape!

The secret:

Nobody saw you

hide a grape in your mouth.

When you toss the other one,

you just pretend to catch it

in your right hand.

You really keep it

in your left hand.

The Flying Glass of Water

Hold up a glass of water.

Cover it with a handkerchief,

and set the glass in a deep pot.

Ask, "Who wants a drink?"

Pick up the glass,

flip off the handkerchief and—

the glass is gone!

57

The secret:

Take a plastic top from a coffee can.

Ask a grown-up to cut it

so it fits the mouth of the glass.

Tape the plastic on the handkerchief.

When you cover the glass,

set the plastic over the mouth.

Do not really pick up the glass—

just the plastic and handkerchief.

It seems you are holding the glass.

58

"Where is the glass?" you ask.

Say, "The glass is flying around.

Here it comes back!

Now it is back in the pot again."

Cover the glass as you did before.

This time, really pick it up.

Flip the handkerchief off and say,

"Here is the flying glass of water.

Who wants a drink?"

Milk in a Hat

You put a paper cup in a hat.

Then you take it out

and pour milk into the hat.

"Oh, dear!" you say.

"I made a mistake!

I will try again."

You put the cup back in the hat

and take it right out.

Surprise! The cup is full of milk!

The secret:

Use two paper cups.

Cut the bottom off one

and fit it inside the other.

Take out the one that has no bottom.

Leave the other cup in the hat

and pour milk into it.

Then set the cup without a bottom

into the full cup

and lift out both together.

Bag of Surprises

Show a paper bag. It is empty.

Then reach into the bag and pull out

a present for everybody—

ribbons, pictures, a handkerchief.

63

The secret:

There are really two bags,

one inside the other.

The inside bag is empty.

The presents are under it

in the other bag.

Your friends take their presents

and say,

"What a great show!"